The Essential
Anti
Inflammatory
Diet Cookbook

Budget-Friendly Anti-Inflammatory
Diet Recipes To Stretch Your Dollar
While Reaching Your Weight Loss
Goals

Miriam Boonen

TABLE OF CONTENTS

INTRODUCTION

Before we discuss the anti-inflammatory diet, let's discuss what inflammation is. Inflammation is the process of your body's immune system reacting to a physical or chemical injury from part of the body. When inflammation is contained, it is usually not harmful to your body. However, sometimes when it goes too long or becomes too severe, it can damage tissue or cause permanent damage to your organs.

By reducing inflammation in your body, you can reduce your chance of experiencing pain and damage from it. By reducing systemic inflammation, like that associated with chronic pain, there are also several benefits in general. These benefits include slowing or preventing the aging process and regulating your weight.

An anti-inflammatory diet is a diet rich in vegetables, omega-3's, and essential nutrients. The diet is designed to balance the body's immune system by including plenty of antioxidants and other natural substances that have an anti-inflammatory effect on the body.

The foods that are rich in anti-inflammatory nutrients include red onions, turmeric, garlic, ginger, eggplant, alfalfa sprouts and tomatoes. Also include salmon and sardines as part of your diet. Other choices include peanut butter, green tea, flax seeds and fish oil.

According to the National Cancer Institute, inflammation can be caused by a multitude of factors including stress, poor diet, smoking, lack of exercise and even certain medications.

In addition to providing relief from many different health issues this diet is also an excellent weight loss program that will help you lose weight quicker than any other diet program because it regulates your appetite.

It provides many different health benefits along with weight loss because it regulates the body's metabolism and helps to halt sugar cravings.

There are many different reasons why you should consider following an anti-inflammatory diet.

This diet can be beneficial for anyone who wants to reduce inflammation in their body and also lose weight.

The anti-inflammatory diet is by far the best weight loss program that you can start to lose weight without doing any exercise and it will help you lose more weight than any other diet program. An anti-inflammatory diet is a ketogenic diet which means that your body will burn fat for energy instead of carbohydrates.

It helps you to lose weight because it lowers the levels of insulin in your body which will reduce or halt sugar cravings.

An anti-inflammatory diet is a diet rich in vegetables, omega-3's, and essential nutrients. The diet is designed to balance the body's inflammatory response by including plenty of antioxidants and other natural substances that have an anti-inflammatory effect on the body.

The foods that are rich in anti-inflammatory nutrients include red onions, turmeric, garlic, ginger, eggplant, alfalfa sprouts and tomatoes. Also include salmon and sardines as part of your diet. Other choices include peanut butter, green tea, flax seeds and fish oil.

According to the National Cancer Institute, inflammation can be caused by a multitude of factors including stress, poor diet, smoking, lack of exercise and even certain medications.

In addition to providing relief from many different health issues this diet is also an excellent weight loss program that will help you lose weight quicker than any other diet program because it regulates your appetite.

It provides many different health benefits along with weight loss because it regulates the body's metabolism and helps to halt sugar cravings.

It helps you to lose weight because it lowers the levels of insulin in your body which will reduce or halt sugar cravings.

The anti-inflammatory diet is by far the best weight loss program that you can start to lose weight without doing any exercise and it will help you lose more weight than any other diet program.

How Much Does Inflammation Affect Your Health?

If you think that inflammation is just a nuisance, think again! It is estimated that almost half of all health-related disease can be attributed to inflammation. Researchers estimate that over 90% of aging is directly related to inflammation.

Even though many people are aware of the connection between inflammation and illness, they still don't do anything about it. This is a problem because chronic inflammation is a root cause for most chronic diseases such as heart disease, arthritis, cancer, diabetes and more.

How to Avoid Inflammation?

You can avoid inflammation by eating anti-inflammatory foods every day. These foods should make up the majority of your diet because they are extremely healthy and help to protect against inflammation.

1. Foods that Reduce Inflammation with Vitamins A and E

Vitamin A is a very important nutrient because it plays a vital role in strengthening the immune system, developing eyesight, and improving reproductive health. Vitamin A can also be used to help prevent cancer and heart disease. It is best to get vitamin A from natural sources like fruits and vegetables rather than using supplements or multivitamins that contain this nutrient.

Vitamin E is another natural vitamin that helps protect against inflammation. This vitamin has powerful antioxidant properties and helps keep the protective sheath on nerve cells healthy. A deficiency of Vitamin E has been found to be a risk factor for several serious conditions including cancer, heart disease, and Alzheimer's disease.

2. Foods that Reduce Inflammation with Carotenoids

Carotenoids are natural pigments that give fruits and vegetables their reds, greens, yellows, and oranges colors. These pigments have been found to be extremely effective at protecting against inflammation. Examples of carotenoids include lycopene and beta-carotene.

3. Foods that Reduce Inflammation with Fiber

Fiber is very important for good health. It helps to detoxify the body and cleanse the digestive tract. Fiber also helps to stabilize blood sugar levels, reduce cholesterol levels, and reduces the risk of inflammatory bowel disease. Foods high in fiber include oats, wheat bran, whole-grain bread and cereals, brown rice, vegetables like broccoli and Brussels sprouts.

4. Foods that Reduce Inflammation with Omega-3 Fatty Acids

Omega-3 fatty acids are extremely important for health. They play an important role in keeping the health of eyesight and brain. They also help to fight inflammation by lowering blood pressure levels and cholesterol levels. The most common sources of omega-3 fatty acids are fish, flax seed oil, and walnuts.

5. Foods that Reduce Inflammation with Chlorophyll

Chlorophyll is a natural pigment in plants that gives them their green color. It has powerful anti-inflammatory properties that can help prevent symptoms of arthritis and gout. Chlorophyll is also very effective at lowering blood pressure levels as well as preventing blood sugar from becoming too high or too low. Chlorophyll is also very effective at fighting free radical damage and preventing many common diseases.

6. Foods that Reduce Inflammation with Flavonoids

Flavonoids are powerful antioxidants that prevent inflammation in the body. They have been shown to help reduce risk of cancer, heart disease, arthritis, and many other conditions. Many foods such as blueberries, apples, blackcurrants and strawberries contain flavonoids which help protect against inflammation.

7. Foods that Reduce Inflammation with Fiber

Fiber is an important nutrient for health and there are two types of fiber; soluble and insoluble. Soluble fiber is found in many foods such as oatmeal, apples, barley, and beans. It can help lower cholesterol levels and stabilize blood sugar levels in the body. Insoluble fiber is found in whole-grain breads, cereals, beans, seeds and fruits. This type of fiber helps to cleanse the digestive tract as well as eliminate toxins through the large intestine.

BREAKFAST

1. Cherry Smoothie

Preparation Time: 5 Minutes

Cooking Time: 2 Minutes

Servings: 1

Ingredients:

- ½ cup Cherries, pitted & frozen
- ½ of 1 Banana, frozen
- 10 oz. Almond Milk, unsweetened
- 1 tbsp. Almonds
- 1 Beet, small & quartered

Directions:

1. To make this delightful smoothie, you need to blend all the ingredients in a high-speed blender for 3 minutes or until smooth.
2. Pour to a serving glass and enjoy it.

Tip: If you wish, you can add one more beet to it.

Nutrition: Calories: 208Kcal Proteins: 5.2g Carbohydrates: 34.4g Fat: 7.1g

2. Gingerbread Oatmeal

Preparation Time: 10 Minutes

Cooking Time: 30 Minutes

Servings: 4

Ingredients:

- ¼ tsp. Cardamom, grounded
- 4 cups Water
- ¼ tsp. Allspice
- 1 cup Steel Cut Oats
- 1/8 tsp. Nutmeg
- 1 ½ tbsp. Cinnamon, grounded
- ¼ tsp. Ginger, grounded
- ¼ tsp. Coriander, grounded
- Maple Syrup, if desired
- ¼ tsp. Cloves

Directions:

1. First, place all the ingredients in a large saucepan over medium-high heat and stir well.
2. Next, cook them for 6 to 7 minutes or until cooked.
3. Once finished, add the maple syrup.
4. Top it with dried fruits of your choice if desired.
5. Serve it hot or cold.

Tip: Avoid those spices which you don't prefer.

Nutrition: Calories: 175Kcal Proteins: 6g Carbohydrates: 32g Fat: 32g

3. Roasted Almonds

Preparation Time: 5 minutes

Cooking Time: 10 minutes

Servings: 32

Ingredients:

- 2 cups whole almonds
- 1 tablespoon chili powder
- ½ teaspoon ground cinnamon
- ½ teaspoon ground cumin
- ½ teaspoon ground coriander
- Salt and freshly ground black pepper, to taste
- 1 tablespoon extra-virgin organic olive oil

Directions:

1. Preheat the oven to 350 degrees F. Line a baking dish with a parchment paper.
2. In a bowl, add all ingredients and toss to coat well.
3. Transfer the almond mixture into prepared baking dish in a single layer.
4. Roast for around 10 minutes, flipping twice inside the middle way.
5. Remove from oven and make aside to cool down the completely before serving.
6. You can preserve these roasted almonds in airtight jar.

Nutrition: Calories: 62, Fat: 5g, Carbohydrates: 12g, Protein: 2g, Fiber 6g

4. Roasted Pumpkin Seeds

Preparation Time: 10 minutes

Cooking Time: 20 minutes

Servings: 4

Ingredients:

- 1 cup pumpkin seeds, washed and dried
- 2 teaspoons garam masala
- 1/3 teaspoon red chili powder
- ¼ teaspoon ground turmeric
- Salt, to taste
- 3 tablespoons coconut oil, meted
- ½ tablespoon fresh lemon juice

Directions:

1. Preheat the oven to 350 degrees F.
2. In a bowl, add all ingredients except lemon juice and toss to coat well.
3. Transfer the almond mixture right into a baking sheet.
4. Roast approximately twenty or so minutes, flipping occasionally.
5. Remove from oven and make aside to cool completely before serving.
6. Drizzle with freshly squeezed lemon juice and serve.

Nutrition: Calories: 136 Fat: 4g, Carbohydrates: 15g, Fiber: 9g, Protein: 25g

5. Roasted Chickpeas

Preparation Time: 10 minutes

Cooking Time: one hour

Servings: 8-10

Ingredients:

- 3 cups canned chickpeas, rinsed and dried
- 2 tablespoons nutritional yeast
- 1 tablespoon ground turmeric
- ½ teaspoon garlic powder
- Pinch of cayenne pepper.
- Salt and freshly ground black pepper, to taste
- 2 tablespoons extra-virgin organic olive oil

Directions:

1. Preheat the oven to 400 degrees F.
2. In a bowl, add all ingredients except freshly squeezed lemon juice and toss to coat well.
3. Transfer the almond mixture right into a baking sheet.
4. Roast for around 1 hour, flipping after every 15 minutes.
5. Remove from oven and keep aside for cooling completely before serving.
6. Drizzle with freshly squeezed lemon juice and serve.

Nutrition: Calories: 190 Fat: 5g, Carbohydrates: 16g, Fiber: 7g, Protein: 12g

6. Spiced Popcorn

Preparation Time: 5 minutes

Cooking Time: 2 minutes

Servings: 2-3

Ingredients:

- 3 tablespoons coconut oil
- ½ cup popping corn
- 1 tbsp. olive oil
- 1 teaspoon ground turmeric
- ¼ teaspoon garlic powder
- Salt, to taste

Directions:

1. In a pan, melt coconut oil on medium-high heat.
2. Add popping corn and cover the pan tightly.
3. Cook, shaking the pan occasionally for around 1-2 minutes or till corn kernels begin to pop.
4. Remove from heat and transfer right into a large heatproof bowl.
5. Add essential olive oil and spices and mix well.
6. Serve immediately

Nutrition: Calories: 200, Fat: 4g, Carbohydrates: 12g, Fiber: 1g, Protein: 6g

7. Cucumber Bites

Preparation Time: 15 minutes

Cooking Time: 0 minutes

Servings: 4

Ingredients:

- ½ cup prepared hummus
- 2 teaspoons nutritional yeast
- ¼-½ teaspoon ground turmeric
- Pinch of red pepper cayenne
- Pinch of salt
- 1 cucumber, cut diagonally into ¼-½-inch thick slices
- 1 teaspoon black sesame seeds
- Fresh mint leaves, for garnishing

Directions:

1. In a bowl, mix together hummus, turmeric, cayenne and salt.
2. Transfer the hummus mixture in the pastry bag and pipe on each cucumber slice.
3. Serve while using garnishing of sesame seeds and mint leaves.

Nutrition: Calories: 203 Fat: 4g, Carbohydrates: 20g, Fiber: 3g, Protein: 8g

8. Spinach Fritters

Preparation Time: 15 minutes

Cooking Time: 5 minutes

Servings: 2-3

Ingredients:

- 2 cups chickpea flour
- ¾ teaspoons white sesame seeds
- ½ teaspoon garam masala powder
- ½ teaspoon red chili powder
- ¼ teaspoon ground cumin
- 2 pinches of baking soda
- Salt, to taste
- 1 cup water
- 12-14 fresh spinach leaves
- Olive oil, for frying

Directions:

1. In a sizable bowl, add all ingredients except spinach and oil and mix till an easy mixture forms.
2. In a sizable skillet, heat oil on medium heat.
3. Dip each spinach leaf in chickpea flour mixture evenly and place in the hot oil in batches.
4. Cook, flipping occasionally for about 3-5 minutes or till golden brown from each side.
5. Transfer the fritters onto paper towel lined plate.

Nutrition: Calories: 211 Fat: 2g, Carbohydrates: 13g, Fiber: 11g, Protein: 9g

9. Crispy Chicken Fingers

Preparation Time: 15 minutes

Cooking Time: 18 minutes

Servings: 4-6

Ingredients:

- 2/3 cup almond meal
- ½ teaspoon ground turmeric
- ½ teaspoon red pepper cayenne
- ½ teaspoon paprika
- ½ teaspoon garlic powder
- Salt and freshly ground black pepper, to taste
- 1 egg
- 1-pound skinless, boneless chicken breasts, cut into strips

Directions:

1. Preheat the oven to 375 degrees F. Line a substantial baking sheet with parchment paper.
2. In a shallow dish, beat the egg.
3. In another shallow dish, mix together almond meal and spices.
4. Coat each chicken strip with egg after which roll into spice mixture evenly.
5. Arrange the chicken strips onto prepared baking sheet in the single layer.
6. Bake for approximately 16-18 minutes.

Nutrition: Calories: 236 Fat: 10g, Carbohydrates: 26g, Fiber: 5g, Protein: 37g

10. Quinoa & Veggie Croquettes

Preparation Time: 15 minutes

Cooking Time: 9 minutes

Servings: 12-15

Ingredients:

- 1 tbsp. essential olive oil
- ½ cup frozen peas, thawed
- 2 minced garlic cloves
- 1 cup cooked quinoa
- 2 large boiled potatoes, peeled and mashed
- ¼ cup fresh cilantro leaves, chopped
- 2 teaspoons ground cumin
- 1 teaspoon garam masala
- ¼ teaspoon ground turmeric
- Salt and freshly ground black pepper, to taste
- Olive oil, for frying

Directions:

1. In a frying pan, heat oil on medium heat.
2. Add peas and garlic and sauté for about 1 minute.
3. Transfer the pea mixture into a large bowl.
4. Add remaining ingredients and mix till well combined.
5. Make equal sized oblong shaped patties from your mixture.
6. In a large skillet, heat oil on medium-high heat.
7. Add croquettes and fry for about 4 minutes per side.

Nutrition: Calories: 367 Fat: 6g, Carbohydrates: 17g, Fiber: 5g, Protein: 22g

LUNCH

11. Lemony Mackerel

Preparation Time: ten minutes

Cooking Time: 15 minutes

Servings 4

Ingredients:

- 1 tablespoon minced chives
- 2 tablespoons olive oil
- 4 mackerels
- Juice of 1 lemon
- Pinch black pepper
- Pinch of sea salt
- Zest of 1 lemon

Directions:

1. Warm a pan with the oil on moderate to high heat, put in the mackerel and cook for about six minutes on each side. Put in the lemon zest, lemon juice, chives, salt, and pepper then cook for two more minutes on each side. Split everything between plates before you serve.
2. Enjoy!

Nutrition: Calories: 289 Cal, Fat::20 g, Fiber: 0 g, Carbohydrates: 1 g, Protein: 21 g

12. Lemony Trout

Preparation Time: ten minutes

Cooking Time: 20 minutes

Servings 2

Ingredients:

- 1 lemon
- 1 tsp. rosemary
- 2 garlic cloves
- 2 tbsp. capers
- 5 oz. trout fillets
- 5 tbsp. ghee butter
- Salt and pepper to taste

Directions:

1. Preheat your oven to 400F
2. Peel the lemon, mince the garlic cloves and cut the capers
3. Flavor the trout fillets with salt, rosemary, and pepper
4. Grease a baking dish with the oil and put the fish onto it
5. Warm the butter in a frying pan on moderate heat
6. Put in the garlic and cook for 4-5 minutes until golden
7. Turn off the heat, put in the lemon zest and 2 tablespoons of lemon juice, stir thoroughly
8. Pour the lemon-butter sauce over the fish and top with the capers
9. Bake for 14-fifteen minutes. Serve hot

Nutrition: Carbohydrates: 3,1 g , Fat: 25 g , Protein: 15,8 g , Calories: 302

13. Lime Cod Mix

Preparation Time: ten minutes

Cooking Time: 15 minutes

Servings 4

Ingredients:

- ½ cup chicken stock
- ½ teaspoon cumin, ground
- 1 tablespoon olive oil
- 2 tablespoons lime juice
- 2 teaspoons lime zest, grated
- 3 tablespoons cilantro, chopped
- 4 cod fillets, boneless
- A pinch of salt and black pepper

Directions:

1. Set the instant pot on Sauté mode, put oil, heats it, put in the cod and cook for a minute on each side.
2. Put in the rest of the ingredients, put the lid on, and cook on High for 13 minutes.
3. Release the pressure naturally for around ten minutes, split the mix between plates before you serve.

Nutrition: Calories 187, Fat: 13.1, Fiber: 0.2, Carbohydrates: 1.6, Protein: 16.1

14. Mackerel Bombs

Preparation Time: 15 minutes

Cooking Time: ten minutes

Servings 4

Ingredients:

- ¼ cup spinach, chopped
- ½ tsp. thyme
- 1 egg, beaten
- 1 tsp. chili flakes
- 1 tsp. garlic, minced
- 1 tsp. mustard
- 1 tsp. salt
- 1 white onion, peeled and diced
- 1/3 cup almond flour
- 10 oz. mackerel, chopped
- 4 tbsp. coconut oil

Directions:

1. Put mackerel in blender or food processor and pulse until texture is smooth.
2. In a container, mix onion with mackerel.
3. Put in garlic, flour, egg, thyme, salt, and mustard, stir thoroughly.
4. Put in chili flakes and mix up the mixture until get homogenous mass.
5. Put in spinach and stir.
6. Heat a pan at moderate heat then put in oil.
7. Shape fish mixture into bombs 1½ inch in diameter.

8. Put bombs on a pan and cook for five minutes on all sides.
9. Move to paper towels and drain grease and serve.

Nutrition: Calories 318, Carbs: 3.45g, Fat: 26.5g, Protein: 20.1g

15. Simply Sautéed Flaky Fillet

Preparation Time: 2 minutes

Cooking Time: 8 minutes

Servings: 6

Ingredients:

- 6-fillets tilapia
- 2-Tbsp.s olive oil
- 1-pc lemon, juice
- Salt and pepper to taste
- ¼-cup parsley or cilantro, chopped

Directions:

1. Sauté tilapia fillets with olive oil in a medium-sized skillet placed over medium heat. Cook for 4 minutes on each side until the fish flakes easily with a fork.
2. Add salt and pepper to taste. Pour the lemon juice to each fillet.
3. To serve, sprinkle the cooked fillets with chopped parsley or cilantro.

Nutrition: Calories: 249 Cal Fat: 8.3 g Protein: 18.6 g Carbs: 25.9 g Fiber: 1 g

16. Zesty Zucchini & Chicken In Classic Santa Fe Stir-Fry

Preparation Time: 5 minutes

Cooking Time: 15 minutes

Servings: 2

Ingredients:

- 1-Tbsp. olive oil
- 2-pcs chicken breasts, sliced
- 1-pc onion, small, diced
- 2-cloves garlic, minced 1-pc zucchini, diced
- ½- cup carrots, shredded
- 1-tsp paprika, smoked 1-tsp cumin, ground
- ½-tsp chili powder ¼-tsp sea salt
- 2-Tbsp. fresh lime juice
- ¼-cup cilantro, freshly chopped
- Brown rice or quinoa, when serving

Directions:

1. Sauté the chicken with olive oil for about 3 minutes until the chicken turns brown. Set aside.
2. Use the same wok and add the onion and garlic.
3. Cook until the onion is tender.
4. Add in the carrots and zucchini.
5. Stir the mixture, and cook further for about a minute.
6. Add all the seasonings into the mix, and stir to cook for another minute.
7. Return the chicken in the wok, and pour in the lime juice.

8. Stir to cook until everything cooks through.
9. To serve, place the mixture over cooked rice or quinoa and top with the freshly chopped cilantro.

Nutrition: Calories: 191 Fat: 5.3g Protein: 11.9g Carbs: 26.3g Fiber: 2.5g

17. Crispy Cheese-Crusted Fish Fillet

Preparation Time: 5 minutes

Cooking Time: 10 minutes

Servings: 4

Ingredients:

- ¼-cup whole-wheat breadcrumbs
- ¼-cup Parmesan cheese, grated
- ¼-tsp sea salt ¼-tsp ground pepper
- 1-Tbsp. olive oil 4-pcs tilapia fillets

Directions:

1. Preheat the oven to 375°F.
2. Stir in the breadcrumbs, Parmesan cheese, salt, pepper, and olive oil in a mixing bowl.
3. Mix well until blended thoroughly.
4. Coat the fillets with the mixture, and lay each on a lightly sprayed baking sheet.
5. Place the sheet in the oven.
6. Bake for 10 minutes until the fillets cook through and turn brownish.

Nutrition: Calories: 255 Fat: 7g Protein: 15.9g Carbs: 34g Fiber: 2.6g

18. Sautéed Shrimp Jambalaya Jumble

Preparation Time: 15 minutes

Cooking Time: 30 minutes

Servings: 4

Ingredients:

- 10-oz. medium shrimp, peeled
- ¼-cup celery, chopped ½-cup onion, chopped
- 1-Tbsp. oil or butter ¼-tsp garlic, minced
- ¼-tsp onion salt or sea salt
- 1/3-cup tomato sauce ½-tsp smoked paprika
- ½-tsp Worcestershire sauce
- 2/3-cup carrots, chopped
- 1¼-cups chicken sausage, precooked and diced
- 2-cups lentils, soaked overnight and precooked
- 2-cups okra, chopped
- A dash of crushed red pepper and black pepper
- Parmesan cheese, grated for topping (optional)

Directions:

1. Sauté the shrimp, celery, and onion with oil in a pan placed over medium-high heat for five minutes, or until the shrimp turn pinkish.
2. Add in the rest of the ingredients, and sauté further for 10 minutes, or until the veggies are tender.
3. To serve, divide the jambalaya mixture equally among four serving bowls.
4. Top with pepper and cheese, if desired.

Nutrition: Calories: 529 Fat: 17.6g Protein: 26.4g Carbs: 98.4g Fiber: 32.3g

DINNER

19. Tender salmon in mustard sauce

Preparation Time: 10 minutes

Cooking Time: 20 minutes

Servings: 2

Ingredients:

- 5 tbsps. Minced dill
- 2/3 c. sour cream
- Pepper.
- 2 tbsps. Dijon mustard
- 1 tsp. garlic powder
- 5 oz. salmon fillets
- 2-3 tbsps. Lemon juice

Directions:

1. Mix sour cream, mustard, lemon juice and dill.
2. Season the fillets with pepper and garlic powder.
3. Arrange the salmon on a baking sheet skin side down and cover with the prepared mustard sauce.
4. Bake for 20 minutes at 390°F.

Nutrition: Calories: 318, Fat: 12 g, Carbs: 8 g, Protein: 40.9 g, Sugars: 909.4 g, Sodium: 1.4 mg

20. Braised Leeks, Cauliflower and Artichoke Hearts

Preparation Time: 10 Minutes

Cooking Time: 10 Minutes

Servings: 4

Ingredients:

- 2 tbsp. coconut oil
- 2 garlic cloves, chopped
- 1 ½ cup artichoke hearts
- 1 ½ cups chopped leeks
- 1 ½ cups cauliflower flowerets

Directions:

1. Heat oil in a skillet over medium high heat.
2. Add the garlic and sauté for one minute. Add the vegetables and stir constantly until the vegetables are cooked.
3. Serve with roasted chicken, fish or pork.

Nutrition: Calories: 111 Fat: 1g Carbohydrates:1 3g Protein: 3g Sugar: 2g Fiber: 4g

21. Scallops Stew

Preparation Time: 10 Minutes

Cooking Time: 20 Minutes

Servings: 4

Ingredients:

- 2 leeks, chopped
- 2 tablespoons olive oil
- 1 teaspoon chopped jalapeno
- 2 teaspoons chopped garlic
- A pinch of salt and black pepper
- ¼ teaspoon ground cinnamon
- 1 carrot, chopped
- 1 teaspoon ground cumin
- 1½ cups chopped tomatoes
- 1 cup veggie stock
- 1-pound shrimp, peeled and deveined
- 1-pound sea scallops
- 2 tablespoons chopped cilantro

Directions:

1. Heat up a pot with the oil over medium heat, add garlic and leeks, stir and cook for 7 minutes. Add jalapeno, salt, pepper, cayenne, carrots, cinnamon and cumin, stir and cook for 5 more minutes.
2. Add tomatoes, stock, shrimp and scallops, stir, cook for 6 more minutes then divide into bowls, sprinkle cilantro on top and serve.
3. Enjoy!

Nutrition: Calories: 251 Cal Fat 4 g Fiber: 4 g Carbs: 11 g Protein: 17 g

22. Spicy baked fish

Preparation Time: 5 minutes

Cooking Time: 15 minutes

Servings: 5

Ingredients:

- 1 tbsp. olive oil
- 1 tsp. spice salt free seasoning
- 1 lb. salmon fillet

Directions:

1. Preheat the oven to 350F.
2. Sprinkle the fish with olive oil and the seasoning.
3. Bake for 15 min uncovered.
4. Slice and serve.

Nutrition: Calories: 192, Fat: 11 g, Carbs: 14.9 g, Protein: 33.1 g, Sugars: 0.3 g, Sodium: 505.6 mg

23. Ambrosial Avocado & Salmon Salad in Lemon-Dressed Layers

Preparation Time: 10-minutes

Cooking Time: 0 Minutes

Servings: 4

Ingredients:

- For the Avocado & Salmon Salad:
- 6-oz wild salmon
- 1-pc avocado, pitted, peeled, and diced
- 2-cups loosely packed salad greens
- ½-cup Monterey Jack cheese, reduced-fat, shredded
- ¾-cup tomato, chopped
- 1-Tbsp lemon juice, freshly squeezed
- For the Lemon Dressing:
- 1 Tbsp. lemon juice, freshly squeezed
- 1 Tbsp. olive oil, extra-virgin
- 1 tsp. honey
- 1/8-tsp. Kosher or sea salt
- 1/8-tsp. black pepper
- ½-tsp Dijon mustard
- 4-units jars

Directions:

1. Combine and whisk all the dressing ingredients excluding the olive oil in a small mixing bowl. Mix well.
2. Drizzle gradually with the oil into the dressing mixture, and keep whisking while pouring.

3. Pour the dressing as to distribute evenly into each jar. Distribute uniformly into each jar similar amounts of the following ingredients in this order: diced tomatoes, cheese, avocado, salmon, and lettuce.
4. Secure each jar by with its lid, and chill the jars in the fridge until ready for serving.

Nutrition: Calories: 267 Cal Fat: 7.4 g Protein: 16.6 g Carbs: 38.1 g Fiber: 4.8 g

24. Steamed fish balls

Preparation Time: 5 minutes

Cooking Time: 25 minutes

Servings: 2

Ingredients:

- 2 whisked eggs
- 2 tbsps. Rinsed and cooked rice
- Salt.
- 10 oz. minced white fish fillets

Directions:

1. Combine the minced fish with the rice.
2. Add eggs, season with salt and stir well.
3. Form the balls. Arrange in a steamer basket.
4. Place the basket in a pot with 1 inch of water.
5. Steam, covered, for 25 minutes or until soft.

Nutrition: Calories: 169, Fat: 4.3 g, Carbs: 1.1 g, Protein: 5.3 g, Sugars: 0 g, Sodium: 173.1 mg

25. Roasted Vegetables with Polenta

Preparation Time: 5 minutes

Cooking Time: 25 minutes

Servings: 6

Ingredients:

- 2 tsp. oregano
- 10 ripe olives, chopped
- 6 dry-packed sun-dried tomatoes, soaked in water to rehydrate, drained and chopped
- 2 plum or Roma tomatoes, sliced
- 10-oz frozen spinach, thawed
- ¼ tsp. cracked black pepper
- 2 tsp. trans-free margarine
- 1 ½ cups coarse polenta
- 6 cups water
- 2 tbsp. + 1 tsp. extra virgin olive oil
- 1 sweet red pepper, seeded, cored and cut into chunks
- 6 medium mushrooms, sliced
- 1 small green zucchini, cut into ¼-inch slices
- 1 small yellow zucchini, cut into ¼-inch slices
- 1 small eggplant, peeled and cut into ¼-inch slices

Directions:

1. Grease a baking sheet and a 12-inch circle baking dish, position oven rack 4-inches away from heat source and preheat broiler.
2. With 1 tbsp. olive oil, brush red pepper, mushrooms, zucchini and eggplant. Place in prepared baking sheet

in a single layer. Pop in the broiler and broil under low setting.

3. Turn and brush again with oil the veggies after 5 minutes. Continue broiling until veggies are slightly browned and tender.
4. Wash and drain spinach. Set aside.
5. Preheat oven to 350oF.
6. Bring water to a boil in a medium saucepan.
7. Whisk in polenta and lower fire to a simmer. For 5 minutes, cook and stir.
8. Once polenta no longer sticks to pan, add 1/8 tsp. pepper and margarine. Mix well and turn off fire.
9. Evenly spread polenta on base of prepped baking dish. Brush tops with olive oil and for ten minutes bake in the oven.
10. When done, remove polenta from oven and keep warm.
11. With paper towels remove excess water from spinach. Layer spinach on top of polenta followed by sliced tomatoes, olives, sun-dried tomatoes, and roasted veggies. Season with remaining pepper and bake for another 10 minutes.
12. Remove from oven, cut into equal servings and enjoy.

Nutrition: Calories 135 Fat 2g Carbohydrates: 27g Protein 5g Fiber: 6g

26. Broccoli-Sesame Stir-Fry

Preparation Time: 10 Minutes

Cooking Time: 8 Minutes

Servings: 4

Ingredients:

- 2 tablespoons extra-virgin olive oil
- 1 teaspoon sesame oil
- 4 cups broccoli florets
- 1 tablespoon grated fresh ginger
- ¼teaspoon sea salt
- 2 garlic cloves, minced
- 2 tablespoons toasted sesame seeds

Directions:

1. In a large nonstick skillet over medium-high heat, heat the olive oil and sesame oil until they shimmer.
2. Add the broccoli, ginger, and salt. Cook for 5 to 7 minutes, stirring frequently, until the broccoli begins to brown.
3. Add the garlic. Cook for 30 seconds, stirring constantly.
4. Remove from the heat and stir in the sesame seeds.

Nutrition: Calories: 134 Fat: 11g Carbohydrates: 9g Sugar: 2g

27. Creamy Cauliflower Parsnip Mash

Preparation Time: 4 minutes

Cooking Time: 25 minutes

Servings: 5

Ingredients:

- 1 Medium-Sized Cauliflower
- 2 Parsnips
- 2 Tbsp. Extra Virgin Olive Oil
- 1/2 Tbsp. Salt
- 1/2 Tbsp. Lemon Juice
- 1 Tbsp. Black Pepper
- 5/6 Roasted Garlic Cloves

Directions:

1. Cut the vegetables into small pieces.
2. Boil them for 10 to 15 minutes in medium temperature until fork-tender.
3. Drain the water and mash them in a blender.
4. Add the remaining ingredients with the mash and blend until the mixture is smooth as butter.
5. Add water and add salt if needed making sure that the batter isn't too thick or runny and serve.

Nutrition: Calories: 72 kcal Carbohydrates: 12 g Fat: 0.8 g Protein: 3.7 g

28. Stir-Fried Garlic Chili Beef

Preparation Time: 5 Minutes

Cooking Time: 10 Minutes

Servings: 2

Ingredients:

- 200g Beef Fillet (Sliced)
- 150g Gai Lan (Cut)
- 1 Medium Red Chilli (Seeded, Chopped)
- 1 Tbsp. Sesame Oil
- 4 Large Garlic Cloves (Chopped)
- Soy Sauce
- Toasted Sesame Oil
- Chinese Five-Spice

Directions:

1. Season the beef with soy sauce and spices.
2. Stir-fry garlic in sesame oil before adding the beef.
3. Add the gai lan and chili, frying until wilted.
4. Serve with drizzles of light soy sauce, salt, and sesame oil.

Nutrition: Calories: 192 kcal, Carbohydrates: 2 g, Fat: 8 g Protein: 29 g

SNACKS

29. Bruschetta

Preparation Time: 10 minutes

Cooking Time: 20 Minutes

Servings: 5

Ingredients:

- Bread, whole-grain – 10 slices
- Extra virgin olive oil – 4 teaspoons, divided
- Sea salt – 0.25 teaspoon
- Garlic, minced – 2 cloves
- Balsamic vinegar – 1 tablespoon
- Basil, fresh, chopped – 0.33 cup
- Parmesan, grated – 0.25 cup
- Roma tomatoes, seeded and diced – 8
- Black pepper, ground – 0.25 teaspoon

Directions:

1. In a mixing dish, prepare the topping for your bruschetta by combining the tomatoes, Parmesan, basil, garlic, sea salt, balsamic, one teaspoon of olive oil, and black pepper. Once combined, cover the kitchen mixing dish and place it in the fridge to marinate while you move onto the next step.

2. Heat a grill pan for the bruschetta over medium heat on your stovetop, or you can use a gas grill to medium

heat or a charcoal grill until the coals have paled in color.

3. While your grill heats, slice each slice of bread in half, so that you are left with twenty small pieces rather than ten large ones. Using a pastry brush, use the remaining tablespoon of olive oil to brush over the bread slices on both sides.

4. Grill both sides of the bruschetta bread until toasted with visible grill marks and then remove it, adding your chilled brochette toppings and serving immediately.

Nutrition: Calories: 91 kcal, Protein: 4.6 g, Fat: 2.51 g, Carbohydrates: 13.88 g

30. Purple Cabbage Salad with Quinoa And Edamame

Preparation Time: 5 minutes

Cooking Time: 2 Minutes

Servings: 8

Ingredients:

- ½ cup dry quinoa
- 1 (10-ounce) bag frozen shelled edamame
- 1 cup vegetable broth
- ¼ cup reduced-sodium tamari
- ¼ cup natural almond butter
- 3 tablespoons toasted sesame seed oil
- ½ teaspoon pure stevia powder
- 1 head purple cabbage, cored and chopped

Directions:

1. Place the quinoa, edamame, and broth in the inner pot of your Instant Pot. Cook within 2 minutes.
2. Whisk the tamari, almond butter, sesame seed oil, and stevia in a small bowl. Set aside.
3. Fluff the quinoa using a fork, and then transfer the mixture to a large bowl. Allow the quinoa and edamame to cool, and then add the purple cabbage to the bowl and toss to combine.
4. Put the dressing and toss again. Serve.

Nutrition: Calories 220 Fat: 11g Protein: 10g Sodium: 313mg Fiber: 7g Carbohydrates: 21g Sugar: 5g

31. French Toast Sticks

Preparation Time: 10 minutes

Cooking Time: 10 Minutes

Servings: 2

Ingredients:

- ½ teaspoon ground nutmeg
- 1 teaspoon vanilla extract
- 1 teaspoon cinnamon
- ¼ cup almond milk
- 4 slices bread, sliced into sticks

Directions:

1. Line your air fryer basket with parchment paper.
2. Preheat your air fryer to 360 degrees F.
3. Combine all ingredients except bread sticks in a bowl.
4. Dip bread sticks into the mixture.
5. Air fry for 5 minutes.
6. Flip and cook for another 5 minutes.

Nutrition: Calories: 134 kcal, Protein: 3.81 g, Fat: 1.92 g, Carbohydrates: 24.17 g

32. Beef Bites

Preparation Time: 10 minutes

Cooking Time: 15 Minutes

Servings: 4

Ingredients:

- 1 tablespoon lime juice
- 2 tablespoons avocado oil
- 1-lb. beef stew meat, cubed
- 2 garlic cloves, minced
- 1 cup beef stock

Directions:

1. Start by adding oil and meat to a cooking pan, then sauté for 5 minutes.
2. Stir in remaining ingredients and mix well
3. Cover the pot's lid and cook for 30 minutes on medium heat.
4. Serve fresh and enjoy.

Nutrition: Calories 142 Total Fat 8.4 g Cholesterol 743 mg Sodium 346 mg Total Carbs 3.4 g Sugar 1 g Fiber 0.8 g Protein 4.1 g

33. Garlic Chili Edamame

Preparation Time: 5 minutes

Cooking Time: 15 Minutes

Servings: 4

Ingredients:

- Edamame – 1 pound
- Sesame seed oil – 0.5 teaspoon
- Extra virgin olive oil – 2 tablespoons
- Garlic, minced – 3 cloves
- Chili paste – 2 tablespoons
- Date paste – 1 teaspoon
- Sea salt – 1 teaspoon

Directions:

1. Head a large skillet over medium-high heat and wait for it to warm up before adding in your edamame. Allow your edamame to sear undisturbed until the bottom sides are charred, and then give them a light stir. Let the pods cook this way, until both sides are charred and tender. Remove the edamame from the skillet and set it aside.

2. Reduce the heat of the stove to medium and then add in the garlic, allowing it to toast for about thirty seconds. Add in the remaining ingredients, stirring together until combined, and then add back in the charred edamame. Cook the edamame in the sauce for a minute or two before removing it from the heat and serving warm.

Nutrition: Calories: 187 kcal, Protein: 13.16 g, Fat: 9.7 g, Carbohydrates: 15.38 g

34. Chia Pudding with Cashews and Cherries

Preparation Time: 10 minutes

Cooking Time: 0 Minutes

Servings: 4

Ingredients:

- 2 cups almond milk
- ½ cup chia seeds
- 1 teaspoon vanilla extract
- ¼ cup pure maple syrup
- ½ cup chopped cashews, divided
- 1 cup frozen no-added-sugar pitted cherries, thawed, juice reserved, divided

Directions:

1. Combine the almond milk, chia seeds, vanilla, and maple syrup in a bowl. Stir to mix well. Refrigerate overnight.
2. Divide the almond milk mixture in four bowls, then serve with cashews and cherries on top.

Nutrition: calories: 271 fat: 13.9g; protein: 7.1g; carbs: 37.8g; fiber: 6.2g; sugar: 25.0g; sodium: 83mg

35. Pecan and Lime Cheesecake

Preparation Time: 10 minutes

Cooking Time: 0 Minute

Servings: 10

Ingredients:

- 1 cup coconut flakes
- 20 ounces mascarpone cheese, room temperature
- 1 ½ cups pecan meal
- 1/2 cup xylitol
- 3 tablespoons key lime juice

Directions:

1. Combine the pecan meal, 1/4 cup of xylitol, and coconut flakes in a mixing bowl. Press the crust into a parchment-lined spring form pan. Freeze for 30 minutes.
2. Now, beat the mascarpone cheese with 1/4 cup of xylitol with an electric mixer.
3. Beat in the key lime juice; you can add vanilla extract if desired.
4. Spoon the filling onto the prepared crust. Allow it to cool in your refrigerator for about 3 hours. Bon appétit!

Nutrition: Calories: 296Fat: 20gCarbs: 6gProtein: 21gFiber: 3.7g

36. Pecan and Spice Stuffed Apple Bake

Preparation Time: 10 minutes

Cooking Time: 2 Hours

Servings: 5 Apples

Ingredients:

- 5 apples, cored
- ½ cup water
- ½ cup crushed pecans
- ¼ teaspoon ground cloves
- 1 teaspoon ground cinnamon
- ¼ teaspoon ground cardamom
- ½ teaspoon ground ginger
- ¼ cup melted coconut oil

Directions:

1. Peel a thin strip off the top of each apple.
2. Pour the water in the slow cooker, then arrange the apples in the slow cooker, upright.
3. Combine the remaining ingredients in a small bowl. Stir to mix well.
4. Spread the mixture on tops of the apples, then put the slow cooker lid on and cook on high for 2 hours or until the apples are tender.
5. Allow to cool for 15 minutes, then remove the apples from the slow cooker gently and serve warm.

Nutrition: (1 apple) calories: 216; fat: 11.6g; protein: 0g; carbs: 30.1g; fiber: 6.2g; sugar: 21.9g; sodium: 0mg

37. Peach Dip

Preparation Time: 10 minutes

Cooking Time: 0 Minute

Servings: 2

Ingredients:

- ½ cup nonfat: yogurt
- 1 cup peaches, chopped
- A pinch of cinnamon powder
- A pinch of nutmeg, ground

Directions:

1. In a bowl, combine the yogurt while using the peaches, cinnamon and nutmeg.
2. Whisk and divide into small bowls and serve.

Nutrition: Calories: 165Fat: 2gFiber: 3gCarbs: 14gProtein: 13g

38. No-bake Golden Energy Bites

Preparation Time: 10 minutes

Cooking Time: 0 Minutes

Servings: 16

Ingredients:

- 1 cup almond butter
- ¾ cup coconut flakes, unsweetened
- 6 tablespoons protein powder
- 1 teaspoon coconut oil
- ½ teaspoon maple syrup
- 2 teaspoons turmeric

Directions:

1. Combine all fixings until thick dough is formed in a bowl.
2. Place dough in a pan lined with parchment paper and spread evenly.
3. Chill within an hour to set. Remove, and then slice to 16 pieces.

Nutrition: Calories 376 Total Fat 36g Saturated Fat 5g Total Carbs 9g Protein 6g Sugar 5g Fiber: 2g

SOUP AND STEW

39. Eggplant Chickpea Stew

Preparation Time: 30 minutes

Cooking Time: 15 minutes

Servings: 2

Ingredients:

- Eggplant, one peeled and cubed
- Black pepper, one teaspoon
- Chickpeas, fourteen ounce can, drain and rinse
- Tomatoes, one fourteen-ounce can, drained
- Salt, one half teaspoon
- Hot sauce, any brand, one tablespoon
- Rosemary, one teaspoon
- Thyme, one half teaspoon
- Olive oil, three tablespoons
- Garlic powder, two tablespoons
- Cilantro, one tablespoon
- Onion, one diced fine

Directions:

1. Fry the salt, onion, eggplant, garlic, and pepper in the olive oil for five minutes.
2. Pour in the chickpeas, tomatoes, and hot sauce; mix well and simmer for fifteen minutes.

Nutrition: Calories 350, 12 grams protein, 10 grams fat, 16 grams carbs

40. Red Pepper and Tomato Soup

Preparation Time: 15 minutes

Cooking Time: 45 minutes

Servings: 4

Ingredients:

- Red bell peppers, two, seeded and diced
- Tomato paste, two tablespoons
- Tomato, three, clean and dice
- Paprika, ground, one half teaspoon
- Parsley, fresh, chop, one quarter cup
- Black pepper, one teaspoon
- Vegetable Broth, two cups
- Garlic, minced, two tablespoons
- Cayenne pepper, one quarter teaspoon
- Italian seasoning, one half teaspoon
- Olive oil, three tablespoons
- Onion, one medium, cut in quarters
- Salt, one half teaspoon

Directions:

1. Heat oven to 425. Use a large mixing bowl to mix the red pepper, garlic, tomatoes, and onion, with the pepper, salt, and olive oil. Spread the veggies on a lined baking pan and bake uncovered for forty-five minutes.
2. Pour the vegetable broth into a pot and heat it to boiling, and then turn the heat down and add in the roasted veggies. Stir this mixture well and simmer for five minutes and serve.

Nutrition: Calories 150, 14 grams carbs, 4 grams protein, 4 grams fat

41. Tuscany Vegetable Soup

Preparation Time: 15 minutes

Cooking Time: 30 minutes

Servings: 8

Ingredients:

- Tomatoes, two large diced small
- Zucchini, one medium peeled and chopped
- Celery, one half cup chop
- Carrot, one half cup chop
- Yellow onion, one medium diced
- Parsley, fresh chopped for garnish
- Olive oil, three tablespoons
- Salt, one half teaspoon
- Garlic, minced, two tablespoons
- Black pepper, one teaspoon
- Vegetable broth, six cups
- Basil, one tablespoon chop fine
- Kale, two cups chop
- Tomato paste, two tablespoons

Directions:

1. Fry the garlic and the onion in the heated olive oil in a large pan. Then add in the zucchini, celery, and carrots and cook ten minutes, stirring frequently. Mix in the salt, pepper, and tomatoes, and cook two more minutes.

2. Pour in the vegetable broth and the tomato paste and boil. Turn lower the heat and let the mixture simmer for fifteen minutes.
3. Put in the basil and the parsley, then remove the pot from the heat and let the soup sit for ten minutes. Top soup with fresh parsley and serve.

Nutrition in one cup: Calories 225, 6 grams fat, 17 grams protein, 12 grams carbs

42. Cheesy Cauliflower Soup

Preparation Time: 10 minutes

Cooking Time: 20 minutes

Servings: 6

Ingredients:

- Cheddar cheese, grated, eight ounces
- Shallot, one
- Heavy cream, two cups
- Salt, one half teaspoon
- Vegetable stock, two cups
- Garlic, minced, two tablespoons
- Black pepper, one teaspoon
- Olive oil, one tablespoon
- Cauliflower, grated, one large head

Directions:

1. Cook the garlic and the shallot in a large pot with the olive oil. Place the cauliflower in the pot and mix well with the olive oil and cook for five minutes. Add in the vegetable stock and the heavy cream and boil.
2. Cook low for five minutes. Blend in the pepper, salt, and cheese, stirring gently for a minute and serve.

Nutrition: Calories 227, 9 grams carbs, 10 grams protein, 16 grams fat

43. Creole Chicken Gumbo

Preparation Time: 20 minutes

Cooking Time: 25 minutes

Servings: 6

Ingredients:

- Cooked chicken, one cup diced
- Chicken broth, four cups
- Tomatoes, stewed, four regular cans
- Olive oil, three tablespoons
- Green bell pepper, chopped, one half cup
- Okra, fresh, chunked, one cups
- Salt, one teaspoon
- Black pepper, one teaspoon
- Parsley, chopped, two tablespoons

Directions:

1. Cook the okra, onion, and green pepper for ten minutes in the olive oil. Add the tomatoes and broth and boil for fifteen minutes. Add chicken and parsley, stir well and serve.

Nutrition: Calories 227, 19 grams carbs, 3 grams fat, 6 grams protein

44. Quinoa Chili

Preparation Time: 10 minutes

Cooking Time: 30 minutes

Servings:

Ingredients:

- Quinoa, one cup cooked
- Kidney beans, one can rinsed
- Oil, one tablespoon
- Black beans, one can rinsed
- Cilantro, fresh chopped, three tablespoons
- Avocado, one peeled and thin sliced
- Black pepper, one teaspoon
- Garlic, three cloves minced
- Onion, one small diced
- Salt, one teaspoon
- Diced tomatoes, one can
- Tomato sauce, one can fifteen ounce
- Green chilies, canned, five ounces
- Chili powder, one tablespoon
- Cumin, ground, two teaspoons
- Paprika, one teaspoon
- Cayenne pepper, one half teaspoon
- Corn, frozen, one package thawed

Directions:

1. Cook onion and garlic in oil for three minutes. Add quinoa, paprika, cayenne pepper, chili powder, cumin,

tomato sauce, green chilies, tomatoes, and two cups of water.

2. Season with pepper and salt and simmer for thirty minutes. Add corn, cilantro, and beans and heat for five minutes.

Nutrition: Calories 337, 64 grams carbs, 12 grams fiber, 17 grams protein, 3 grams fat

45. Tomato Basil Chicken Stew

Preparation Time: 15 minutes

Cooking Time: 30 minutes

Servings: 4

Ingredients:

- Chicken, three cups diced cooked
- Red pepper flakes, crushed, one quarter teaspoon
- Basil, fresh chopped, one quarter cup
- Canned whole tomatoes, two twenty-eight ounce cans with juice
- Black pepper, one teaspoon
- White beans, one can rinsed
- Salt, one teaspoon
- Olive oil, one tablespoon
- Onion, one small chopped
- Carrots, two, peeled and diced
- Celery, two stalks diced
- Garlic, four cloves minced
- Baby spinach, two cups

Directions:

1. Warm oil in a large pot and add carrots, celery, and onion and cook for ten minutes. Add in the garlic and cook for two minutes.
2. Add the rest of the ingredients and stir well. Boil the mixture, and then simmer for fifteen minutes and serve.

Nutrition: Calories 330, 24 grams carbs, 7 grams fiber, 28 grams protein, 15 grams fat

46. Minestrone

Preparation Time: 20 minutes

Cooking Time: 1 hour

Servings: 8

Ingredients:

- Cheese, Parmesan or Romano, one-quarter cup shredded
- Black pepper, one teaspoon
- Spinach, fresh, baby, four cups
- Basil, one half teaspoon
- Squash, one medium yellow, thin-slice
- Zucchini, one medium, thin-slice
- Carrots, one-half cup diced
- Garlic, minced, four tablespoons
- Onion, white, one small minced
- Pasta shells, whole wheat, small, one cup
- Oregano, two teaspoon
- Water, two cups
- Vegetable broth, four cups
- Olive oil, three tablespoons
- Celery, one-half cup sliced thin
- Thyme, one quarter teaspoon
- Parsley, fresh minced, two tablespoons
- Diced tomatoes, fire-roasted, one fourteen to fifteen ounce can
- Salt, one teaspoon

- Kidney beans, red, two fifteen ounce cans rinse and drain
- Cannellini beans, two fifteen ounce cans rinse and drain

Directions:

1. Cook parsley, celery, zucchini, squash, garlic, carrots, and onion in hot olive oil in a large pot for five minutes, stirring often.
2. Pour in water, diced tomatoes, kidney beans, herbs, salt, pepper, cannellini beans, and broth and stir well to blend flavors.
3. Boil the mix, then lower the heat and simmer for thirty minutes. Drop in the pasta and spinach and simmer for thirty more minutes. Mix in the grated cheese and serve immediately.

Nutrition: Calories 110, 17 grams carbs, 4 grams fiber, 5 grams protein, 1 grams fat

47. Pasta Faggioli

Preparation Time: 10 minutes

Cooking Time: 1 hour 30 minutes

Servings: 8

Ingredients:

- Ditalini pasta, one pound, cooks by package directions
- Parmesan cheese, grated, one third cup
- Garlic, minced, two tablespoons
- Onion, one, peeled and chunked
- Olive oil, three tablespoons
- Navy beans, one fifteen ounce can drain and rinse
- Cannellini beans, one fifteen ounce can drain and rinse
- Salt, one teaspoon
- Oregano, dried, one and one half teaspoons
- Basil, dried, one and one half teaspoons
- Parsley, one tablespoon
- Water, six cups
- Tomato sauce, one twenty-nine ounce can

Directions:

1. Cook the garlic and onion in a large pot in the olive oil for five minutes.
2. Lower the heat and add water, navy beans, cannellini beans, parmesan cheese, parsley, salt, oregano, basil, and tomato sauce, stir well and simmer one hour. Mix in cooked pasta and simmer five more minutes.

Nutrition: Calories 403, 68 grams carbs, 8.4 grams fiber, 16.3 grams protein, 7.6 grams fat

SMOOTHIES

48. Almond and Pear Smoothie

Preparation Time: 10 minutes

Cooking Time: 0 minutes

Servings: 1

Ingredients:

- 2-3 dates, optional
- ¼ tsp. ground cinnamon
- 1 tbsp. unsalted almond butter
- ½ cup almond milk
- ½ pear, deseeded
- 1 banana, frozen

Directions:

1. Add all ingredients in a blender.
2. Blend until smooth and creamy.
3. Serve and enjoy.

Nutrition: Calories 341 Total Fat 11g Saturated Fat 0.8g Total Carbs 62g Net Carbs 53g Protein 6g Sugar: 41g Fiber 9g

49. Berry Nutty Smoothie

Preparation Time: 10 minutes

Cooking Time: 0 minutes

Servings: 1

Ingredients:

- 1 cup frozen mix berries
- ½ cup almond milk
- ¼ cup raw cashews
- ¼ cup quick-cooking oats
- 1 cup packed Romaine lettuce
- ¼ cup packed Swiss chard, packed, chopped and stems discarded
- Ice cubes or cold water - optional

Directions:

1. Add all ingredients in a blender.
2. Blend until smooth and creamy.
3. Serve and enjoy.

Nutrition: Calories 269 Total Fat 10g Carbs 43g Protein 6g Sugar: 25g Fiber 7g Sodium 114mg

50. Pomegranate-Avocado Smoothie

Preparation Time: 10 minutes

Cooking Time: 0 minutes

Servings: 1

Ingredients:

- ½ cup spinach
- ½ cup ice
- ½ tsp. vanilla extract
- ½ tbsp. honey
- ½ cup Pomegranate Juice
- ¼ cup Greek Yogurt
- ½ Avocado, peeled

Directions:

1. Add all ingredients in a blender.
2. Blend until smooth and creamy.
3. Serve and enjoy.

Nutrition: Calories 295 Total Fat 15g Carbs 36g Protein 7g Sugar: 27g Fiber 7g Sodium 46mg Potassium 906mg

51. Oats, Flaxseeds and Banana Smoothie

Preparation Time: 10 minutes

Cooking Time: 0 minutes

Servings: 1

Ingredients:

- ½ cup of ice
- 1 tsp. honey
- 2 tsp. flaxseeds
- ¼ cup 100% whole grain rolled oats
- 1/2 cup Greek Yogurt, plain
- ½ cup almond milk
- ½ banana, peeled
- ¼ cup kale, shredded and stems discarded

Directions:

1. Add all ingredients in a blender.
2. Blend until smooth and creamy.
3. Serve and enjoy.

Nutrition: Calories 305 Total Fat 10g Total Carbs 54g Protein 11g Sugar: 30g Fiber 8g Sodium 147mg

52. Strawberry Smoothie

Preparation Time: 5 minutes

Cooking Time: 0 minute

Servings: 2

Ingredients:

- 300ml Sour Yoghurt
- 200g Frozen Strawberries
- 1 Banana
- 2 Tbsp. Brown Sugar
- 3 Strawberries

Directions:

1. Blend everything.
2. Serve with strawberries.

Nutrition: Calories: 371 kcal Carbs: 51 g Fat: 4.2 g Protein: 1.4 g

53. Avocado Smoothie

Preparation Time: 5 minutes

Cooking Time: 0 minute

Servings: 2

Ingredients:

- 1 Large Avocado (Peeled)
- 1 Cup Golden Milk
- 1/8 Tbsp. Vanilla Extract
- 2 Tbsp. Maple Syrup
- Salt to taste

Directions:

1. Blend everything.
2. Add ice cubes.

Nutrition: Calories: 323.2 kcal Carbs: 29.2 g Fat: 25.1 g Protein: 5.1 g

CONCLUSION:

E ating an anti-inflammatory diet will help you avoid a lot of the health issues related to inflammation. It has been found that if you eat a majority of anti-inflammatory foods, your risk of diabetes, heart disease, and cancer will decrease significantly.

Anti-inflammatory foods contain a variety of key compounds that activate the body's natural healing mechanism. Research studies have found that eating anti-inflammatory foods such as tomatoes, broccoli, red wine, and Brussels sprouts reduces the risk of heart disease by 12% or more. Many other health benefits have been discovered because of these foods.

The anti-inflammatory effects of foods are due to the antioxidant properties of these foods. Antioxidants can protect against free radical damage and inflammation of the body. The body's natural healing mechanism will perform better when you eat foods that have antioxidants in them.

The anti-inflammatory effects of foods can be explained due to their antioxidant properties. Antioxidants protect against free radical damage and inflammation of the body. Antioxidants are very important to your body because they work as a defense mechanism, detoxifying cellular components and protecting against oxidative damage. These foods contain antioxidants that fight free radicals, like beta carotene, vitamin C, and the healthy fat known as omega 3 fatty acid. Foods that have been shown to reduce inflammation include berries, red wine, tomatoes, green tea, berries, garlic, and olive oil.

There is a wide variety of foods that exhibit anti-inflammatory effects. Research studies have shown that these foods increase the production of white blood cells that fight against inflammation. White blood cells can play a key role in fighting disease by producing enzymes and antibodies that help destroy cancerous tumors or heal an infected wound.

I hope these recipes will help you get started on an anti-inflammatory diet. If you like to eat these foods on a regular basis, I encourage you to continue doing so. You will certainly enjoy the health benefits that you will get from these foods.